T0146981

COURAGE
CAN'T BREATHE UNLESS
YOU GIVE IT AIR

The poetry and thoughts that brought her to me

MECHELLE KELLY

authorHOUSE®

AuthorHouse™
1663 Liberty Drive
Bloomington, IN 47403
www.authorhouse.com
Phone: 1 (800) 839-8640

©2019 Mechelle Kelly. All rights reserved.

No part of this book may be reproduced, stored in
a retrieval system, or transmitted by any means
without the written permission of the author.

Published by AuthorHouse 10/10/2019

ISBN: 978-1-7283-2872-0 (sc)
ISBN: 978-1-7283-2871-3 (e)

Library of Congress Control Number: 2019914789

Print information available on the last page.

Any people depicted in stock imagery provided
by Getty Images are models, and such images
are being used for illustrative purposes only.
Certain stock imagery © Getty Images.

This book is printed on acid-free paper.

Because of the dynamic nature of the Internet,
any web addresses or links contained in this book
may have changed since publication and may no
longer be valid. The views expressed in this work
are solely those of the author and do not necessarily
reflect the views of the publisher, and the publisher
hereby disclaims any responsibility for them.

I extend my gratitude to

Pat
Linda
Cassie
Tina
Lulu
Lisa
Warren
and
my cat Yoshi who never left a pen
above floor level for long.
I love you all.

I want to thank Sara Bareilles
for her song 'Brave'.

Preface

I woke in the middle of the night hearing you say, "I believe in you."

I'd been praying before bed, "God, please allow the woman that's best for me and I'm best for her to spend time together, while we sleep, developing a rapport, so when we see each other we flow." I asked for a woman...for whom I bring out her best and she mine. That I am what she wants and she is what I want. Our love is so deep that after I exhale, she breathes. From sleep to life, we learn to love each other and lead with this kind of love.

There is a woman out there who has my name on her heart and hers on mine (not literally). I hope she knows I've heard her and I'm doing my best to write poetry that inspires gravity...because the time we share while we sleep...in our shared dreams...is no longer enough for me.

I do all of this,
every moment,
every dance on top of the tree...
to call you home,
to peel the layers,
to **connect you to me.**

Fear Is An Illusion

We disrobe with such abandon.
We should dress ourselves,
as if no matter what we wear,
they will love us.

PART I

Courage Can't Breathe
Unless You Give It Air

Our connection to our world,
it's about the tender moments
we share ourselves.
It's love.
Be you,
watch the world begin to rotate for you.
Courage can't breathe
unless you...
give it air.

We Love

We love
like the dawn,
learning about each other,
as our hearts awaken to the
infinite we've always shared.

Head On Her Heart

Love has a cadence,
a rhythm,
a sound.
It is a finger that traces,
a song
that sings you to sleep.
You dance with it as you dream.

Step Out Of The Shadows Of Fear

With you
there is no armor.
From day one
it begins to drop away
piece by piece.
I step out of the shadows of fear
into life,
allowing myself to be open to you,
your family,
to loving someone
to the extent that everything I do...
makes us stronger.

Come Winter,
snow on the ground,
we all walk on water.
Each of us is **extraordinary.**
Be brave enough to adjust your focus.
Let go
Live

I Align The Pencil Before My Eye

You are the light
every room looks for.
You are the reason
bees work so diligently.
You are the mountain top
the climber seeks.
You are the place,
person,
feeling that inspires love to grow
and
time to stall in awe.

Life Has Layers

Life has layers,
much like a horizon
as it nears twilight.
The lives you gently touch,
people you encourage,
(like sending a child on her
second try on a bike)
love you give your family.
They add the hue,
tone,
texture.
They make the medium
of your work flow
like ink from the finest of pens.
The bonds,
support,
understanding of friends,
they add structure to the bridge.
They remind you of whom you've been,
whom they truly see.
They are your visionaries
when you are nested in the now,
they remind you
to live intentionally.
All these layers,
they remind us
that we don't have to wait.

We can hear our version
of the stars ring like chimes.
We have the capability
to create that kind of beauty now.

Breadcrumbs

Words are breadcrumbs,
we scatter.
Sharing bits ourselves,
like roots feeding their tree.
Sometimes we're the roots,
sometimes we're the tree.

Her Way

Depth can be
as shallow as the sliver,
yet
as wonderfully complex
as the roots of a tree.

Stars

What if our **stars** are **all** *around* us?
What if *each person* is an *inspiring* **mural**,
we simply need to listen to...
to **truly** *see* the lines,
the c*o*lor
the artist's **intent**?
What if *we took the time*,
a**gain** and a**gain**,
to find these things out?

Dance

You dance in my soul,
whisper on my heart
slide your lips between mine,
til' we become the tide,
the waves,
the ocean.

I am occupied by your words.
They are flavorful,
brilliant and imaginative.
The world expanded...
due to a few
obscure,
delightful,
angular questions.
It's as if you've explained a
work of art that was seen
in black and white,
but contained every color.
I have found love in the deep
mystery of your truth.

Our World Is Our Louvre

Have you ever seen the outside of a building
then walked
inside,
stood in awe,
having discovered its inner beauty?
People are like this,
if you get to know them,
you'll see the swirls,
the dips,
the horizon in their ideas.

How Can We Be Anything But Us?

We might not be what people expect to see,
when they do they are inspired.
Two people,
who build a world around us of love,
thoughtfulness,
encouragement,
belief that everyone
should have a shot at joy,
a reason to smile,
feel accepted,
appreciated,
valued.
We do this,
because that's what love does.
It builds.
It plants.
It waters.
It sits back
watches the harvest,
the celebration,
like two people on the beach,
watching
listening to the ocean waves.

This joy,
purposeful joy,
planted in us,
in others,
it's music to the ear,
the sweetest of scenery.

Scribble Away The Critic

The art of the wave,
foam of the sea,
sound of the motion,
settles the silt of perceived reality.
We each have the power to
re-write our story,
to be who we choose to be.

Wax And Candle Are One

I meld into you,
as you hold me close.
I've given the day,
us,
my heart and soul.
And now
my reason,
you,
are my salve.

Love Needs Room To Breathe

Do you know the color,
word,
melody,
medium...
of what it takes to truly love someone?
Do you have the ratchet set
to reassemble her
after a day where a deep hug,
keeps her from imploding?
Love is the lead.
Sure...she can press on,
but give room for her poise
to let go enough
express her need.
Love too,
needs room to breathe.

Part II

I Am Enough, As Is

What would it take to gulp down fear,
like getting rid of a hiccup
and choose courage?
The courage
it takes to open your jacket,
reveal the hole
and allow someone to see it.
Showing this to someone,
it's like saying a piece of me went missing
are you okay with that?
Do you see why I function
as I function?
Her response,
"I've believe in you.
And while you might have thought
you were incomplete,
I disagree.
You have the most gorgeous
asymmetrical soul."

The Best Seat In the House

Sometimes my soul,
it simply
needs to rest
on hers.

Big Bang

Legend cannot stand alone,
it requires a tender love,
a meticulous hand *and* care,
hearts that open,
as life becomes real
and two stars
begin to take their form.

Self-Doubt

A giant stomped through
with the intent to scare.
The lion stepped up
with a smirk
and
flick of her hair.
The sheen of her muscles,
the growl of beware,
the giant thought better
than to raise the hackles on this lion's hair.

No Glitter Needed

I love the human connection,
the bare faced,
truth,
kindness
that fills the awkward gap,
love,
understanding.
Gently holding a person's soul
recognizing its every sparkle,
especially,
most importantly,
when they thought,
you thought,
it was absent.
The look in your eyes,
tenderness you show,
the opening you give,
confirms
it was more than a mere sparkle-
it was a full on shine.

Love Me Like You Mean It

How do I let someone in,
when I don't know them yet?
I've built this work of art,
me,
truly me.
To trust
that no matter what,
no matter when,
she'll be there for me.
My journey's taught me that
that kind of unconditional,
selfless,
engulfing,
kind,
romantic love
friendship...
it's all I'm capable of having.
After all the oddities I've experienced,
endured
overcome to get here,
the sky should serve her to me,
like peanut butter and honey on warm toast
with the most delicious glass of tea.
Love me like you mean it.

Balance

If I am willing
to see things from your perspective,
hear your heart
find a way to connect
your clarity to my curiosity.
We might find passages
that have never been explored.

You Know It All and You Love Me

There isn't anything,
anyone,
any situation that will
separate you from me.
All I have to do is look up and you've,
once again,
shown me you're here to stay.
It's your heart smarts,
that gets me.

You Did Not Just Say That!

Take me to your world...
you're my **multi-colored** air balloon.
The things only you find **funny,**
those **quirks,**
all you hold dear,
every layer.
Show me **who you are.**
Keep me going.

You'd Never Allow Me To Stagnate

I'm coasting along…
you ask the right questions.
You get me curious.
You make me feel connected
to what can happen,
possibilities,
what I can do,
where we can go with this.
The difference we can make.
No way do you doubt me.
Your subtle inspirations
feed my freedom
and
link our hands,
our future,
your belief in me,
us.
As always,
ever,
I exhale
you take a breath.

Take Courage Love

I know you're looking.
Take courage love.
Time will stand still for us.
It's as if the angels have prepared our table.
These moments,
as we prepare for love,
please know,
there's not a moment I'm not holding you.

Climb A Tree

with me.
Stay there,
looking down at our world.
It belongs to us.
We can make it
anything we want.
We say it all the time,
"I believe in you."
My heart surrounds yours,
protective,
fearless.
There isn't a dawn that breaks,
in which you don't wake
sharing
me with you.
There isn't a tree we can't climb,
making the world ours
again and again.
Share the world with me.

She Kicks The Big Bad Wolf's Butt

We've all had those moments,
when we need a reset.
We all need someone,
our love,
that kiss
on the lips...
that glue...
sets deep in our soul.
That person,
her medicinal properties,
touch
how much she cares,
it feels like it melts the illusion
we were wrestling with.
Like this one person,
by holding us tight,
keeps all we built beautiful.

You silently roar.
It's time for bed.
Forever a night,
I am yours.
We can paint
Picasso's night sky.
We can take
Frost's roads.
We can feel
the sculptor's work,
trace it's grooves,
lines and angles.
It's our dream.
We can go anywhere.
I'll do almost
anything with you,
as long as it's something
that makes you smile,
hold your head high,
sigh,
glow...
and wake-up for another day together.

The Cow Looked Fear In The Eyes, Jumped The Moon And Became A Legend

The stars dropped from strings
like a mobile,
swung back and forth,
like a child's feet from a chair.
This happened
because they were excited…
today
was the day
you were facing your fear
and
your joy.

What if we were each like a clock?

All our parts were disassembled
and only our true,
deepest love
knew the secret
of **our assembly**,
what makes us tick?

I Won't Leave You On An Island

Your walk
is my walk.
Your endurance
my deepest care.
No tear will drop
my roar won't rectify.

Trust

What ally is this
who calls to my heart,
who beckons
the warmest of my smiles?
It is as if
a candle has melted
to reveal deeper colors within.
You refuse to let me go
I'd never ask you to.
I simply adore you.
You give me endless reasons to trust you.

The world just shimmered,
as you looked at me.
Knowing my heart
in a delicate state,
you approached with care.
You came
intent to serve,
I needed you just so.
Your presence
ignited the lamp,
I thought lacked fuel.

Sweet Smile Moving

In this life,
I see good,
I feel hope.
It's love
I set my sights on.
I can skip the filler routines
go straight to love every time.
Heart pumping,
"honey I'm home",
I'd do anything to get your
sweet smile moving.
Love

Sweet Spot

We choose what orbits us,
who brings the sun,
whether we allow that sun in to bless us.
Even on the toughest day,
being brave enough to ask
for what we need,
a hug,
pizza,
a silent hour
we know you're right there.
Sometimes glue is so much more,
the fact that it's in our cabinet,
available,
ready...
it creates that sweet spot.
It confirms
love's volume
can be turned up
when we need it.

How many times have we responded, "good",
when we needed a hug that
lifted us off our feet?
That told us,
no one,
nothing
will stop me from making it right for you?
Time stops for that kind of love.
It nudges the two together,
restarts.
Time is fueled on love.
Without love,
time would lose its significance.
With love,
time is incandescent light,
valuable,
precious,
worth savoring.

In one of our dreams together,
your shadow
walked away with mine.
Revealing that together,
we supply **constant sunshine**.

Feast

The immovable feast of the soul,
love,
you.

0 to 60

Your pulse quickens…

I dropped down
to fill you
with a new reality.
Your cry
met with my kiss,
simple taste of my lips.
I could slide against your wake
a thousand times
wanting more.

The Glass Let Them See Through

A feeling,
a moment,
under glass...
like a butterfly specimen on display.
Imagine
if viewing that kind of art
evoked the emotion itself.
Love
captured,
classified,
identified as,
"I would absorb you and
protect you within me,
if you needed me to."
Anticipation,
pressing against the glass,
like a child peering through.
Kindness,
people stepping up to treat you
like you matter,
the glass let them see through.

Drive Me

Would you drive me to that place
inside,
were only you have access?
When you kiss my lips
osmosis occurs.
You swim in me,
through me,
around me
I breathe in every movement,
every sound,
all the subtleties.
You are like smoke
through the nostrils,
sensuously
finding your way
through me.

Beautiful View

I have lifted the earth
above the sea
for you.
Not to climb,
not for the challenge,
but to give you the most beautiful view.
I've removed your burdens.
Your soul
gave me permission to.
You sleep better.
You allow yourself rest.
You open up to being you.

I want to be crowded with love.
I want to spread my love
like it's the last third of the jar,
"what the heck".
I want to make sure
I tend to every detail,
yet let it ride.
I want to draw my love,
as if there was never an option to hide.

Look Me In The Eyes And Dive In

This moment
my love,
don't hesitate
to pour your heart into me.
Dive off a cliff,
glide past the sea,
stare into the sunlight
brazen,
bold,
carefree.

I am your battery.
The love we share
energizes us.
We're a projector.
When you add the film...
magic happens,
a story begins.
Instead of adapting to our environment,
it adapts to us.
Our energy,
profoundly strong...
swirls and flows,
creating a life.
A life far beyond
what we were told
we could do.

A Tree Is A Mountain

A tree is a mountain
unafraid of being seen
for every limb,
knot,
ring.
Every lesbian,
every woman
should feel this way.
We are spectacular.
Our personalities
lush,
we nourish life
simply with our energy,
our being.
We make love simple.
We stand tall.
We make self-love seen.

Greatness

glides past the storm.
It never worries about which door.
Greatness does not clutch.
It does not hoard.
It flows like the river.
It remembers previous success.
It uses those moments
as stairs to the stars.

The She Lovers Who Heard The Poetry

Who found the beauty
within the gray,
the color
within the dark,
the mountain
within the plain,
the painting
within the blank space?
The she lovers who heard the poetry,
when nothing was said,
acted with courage,
when they thought
they were over their heads.

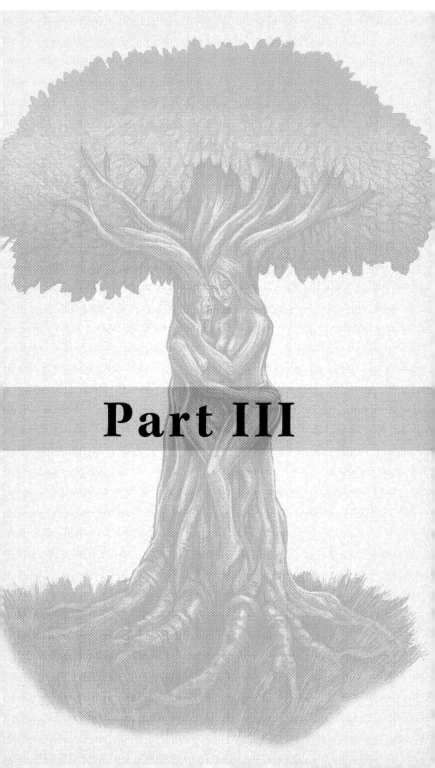

Part III

The Way We Love

There is a definitive moment
when love leaps off the page,
into the now...
trickles down our center line.
It's when all that we hold dear
becomes
all that we both hold dear.
Your favorite jeans are mine to look after,
so they can continue to make
you feel amazing.
You wash my cup with care,
because seeing me peacefully holding it,
gazing out the window...
then into your eyes,
confirms that our life's rhythm
moves the way we love.

One Hour

It has been one hour
since you left bed
I'm just not finished.
My flavorful morning meal,
find the coffee less invigorating
warm your feet on mine.
Confirm to me
there is only one view
in the morning that matters.
Do you realize
your voice
in the morning
connects the dots for me?
No matter what the day holds,
hearing your voice
transforms all that is around me
into an opus.

I Will Love You

I will love you
listen
beyond
the beat of the heart
into your safest secret.

.

Poet's Deepest Love

I'm staying up to write,
you insist I do it in bed.
I've discovered
a new way to write,
according to
the smoothness of your breaths
as you sleep.
It opens a doorway,
reveals a path,
leads me to a fountain.
Words bubble and flow.

I Can Lean Against You

listening to your voice,
thoughts,
stories.
You've never been afraid
of showing me you.
Opening your vast storehouse
ideas,
insights
complete trust in me.
When you show me,
so clearly,
who you are,
you allow us to grow
that much more.
We journey together.
We travel as one,
like the wind over the sea.

The World Is Right

I hear you breathing.
I couldn't sleep,
the world is right.
Your leg has claimed mine
once again.
I check on our cat,
she's right too.
Love,
it's the oxygen,
nutrients,
it gives my feet solid ground,
certainty.

Love lasts,
when you open the door,
allowing her to see it all.
Love grows,
when you're you
without apology.
Love stays,
when you dig in loyally,
faithfully.
You show up,
all in,
no matter what.
You stay,
you discover
every quirk,
the deepest scar...
to you,
they are the grandest texture,
the most beautiful groove,
a graceful curve.
Love knows no erosion.
Loves' infinite imprint is flawless.

Alchemy

What if the story,
pattern of our DNA
could be reconfigured?
What if the brain,
concepts,
preconceived notions,
could be reworked
like a theorem?
What if
we didn't have to go
to the molecular level,
it came to us?
What if we could activate gravity
with our imagination,
creating
a different reality?
What if
we looked at love
like paint?
The more layers
we apply to our lives,
in various forms,
the more profound its effect.
What if
we examined the time
effort
we took in applying love,

inspiring love,
participating in love...
and
woke to the truth...
We're all alchemists.

Early To Bed

That electric moment
where you move close...
the world *always* disappears.
You right the roller coaster,
you settle the waves,
your, "I love you like the owl
loves the tootsie center."
That silly,
relieving sense of humor
that nuzzles my neck while saying it,
I could use
right now.
Shadows disappear faster
when we combine our light.
You're the reason
I go to bed early sometimes.

The Edge

Love is the edge of a cliff
with a giggle.
Either way,
it's the beginning of something.

I've told you everything.
You look at me
as if I'd saved a child
from a burning building.
In some ways I did.
In my honesty,
you moved closer to love me.
I didn't pretend,
which was exactly
what released your story,
our all night conversations.
Your humor
our deepest understanding.
We have no barriers.
We didn't make excuses.
We didn't create a cover.
We stood tall,
naked,
honest,
certain who we are.

I Write Beautiful On Your Hand

Our souls speak words,
cryptic and true,
sculpting us,
joining us,
layering us.
Words are our algorithm
our formula,
font.
One word could change it all.

I Built Us A Home

I have this tattoo.
At the time,
I thought it was a mistake.
The artist transposed the symbol,
so he tattooed one like it,
facing the first.
Later,
I covered it with a tree.
I think I built us a home,
a sanctuary.
You've been with me,
living with me for years.
Evidence that I'm with you...
your eyelashes.
Who else do you think would
love you more than I...
the one who's always there to
wipe away any tears.
Always the first thing you
see in the morning,
the last at night.

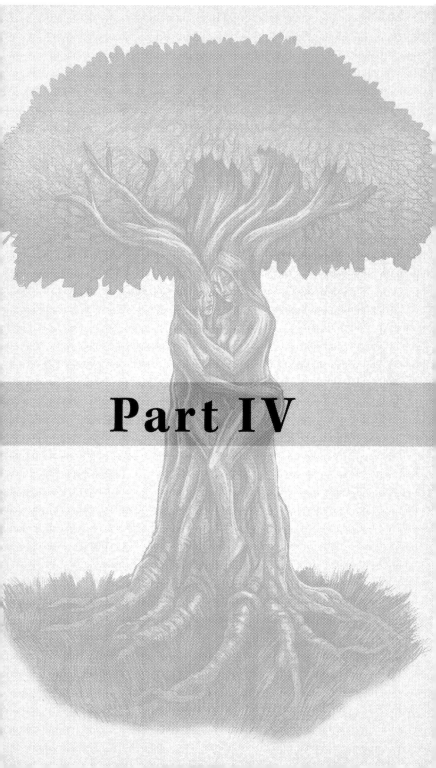

Part IV

Self = Awareness

Second grade,
the two cutest,
adventurous little girls.
My friend showed me
her brother's 'magazine' collection.
Story was he only read
them for the 'articles'.
We appreciated
the artwork called woman.
It's one of my most hilarious and
truth telling lesbian moments.
When we set children free
to be who they are,
they don't hide in rooms,
closets
to catch a glimpse.
They share love,
a magical,
joyous,
engulfing energy.

The Same Air As You

At two and a half,
I'd climb 60 foot trees,
high in the sky
as I could go.
My dad occasionally tells this story,
thinking it was sheer courage.
I know the truth.
I had my heart on my sleeve.
The woman I loved hadn't been born yet.
It's the closest I could get,
very best I could do...
to breath the same air as you.

The Bright Side

Age ten,
I believe I was the first girl
in the state to wrestle.
My mom had me compete in
'her' version of a singlet...
a multi-colored mosaic,
one piece
swimsuit...
Kelly green cotton tights
textured pattern
red waffle bottom sneakers.
The gymnasiums were usually packed.
I had to march out in front of the crowd,
make my moves,
win.
Forty years later,
you walk in,
the most beautiful smile I've ever seen...
momentarily,
my ten year old nervous knees are back.
I will definitely remember to thank
my mom in heaven one day.

She Writes The River For Me

She writes the river for me,
makes it go on and on
to express her love indefinitely.
It fuels the ocean,
tastes the sea.
Dives through the current
to get to me.

I'm going to enjoy this.
I did it!
I shape my destiny.
Holy sh*t, I'm so cool!
I'm so proud of myself.
I can do this!
I am brilliant!
I love myself.
Our words can take us wherever we want to go.

Together

I see you again.
You jump into my arms,
wrap your beautiful legs around me
whisper in my ear,
"You can do this! Make it last."
You kiss my bottom lip,
a bit of a tug,
playful smile.
This kind of love,
every drop...
that kind of embrace,
buzzes through my system
and I'm certain...
the world breathes better
when we're together.

liberty

liberty removes rules
punctuations
measures
guidelines
liberty has no master
but itself
ride who you are
like a raft
on white water
fearlessly

Love who you are,
every moment of who you are,
like that favorite picture of yourself.
The person in the picture is you...
that's why you love it so much.

The Seam

I am latitude.
You are longitude.
At the point where we cross,
there is a seam in the sky.
It leaks love...
drifting down,
like falling leaves.

Sound Stood Still

It hung in the air,
like a monkey in a tree.
Watching our dance,
two souls,
earth-bound stars
in complete harmony.

My Wings

I am opening.
Sometimes,
as this occurs,
it looks more like I'm getting a wedgie
than smiling.
My coping mechanism,
to sketch the world around me
through poetry,
imagery.
It's my wings,
air balloon.
It removes the ceiling,
balances the floor.

Right Where I Want To Be

I pace back and forth,
cloud to cloud by day.
I listen to the stars
by night
ride the notes,
songs.
They might not always be in tune...
they hold beauty
like a pot
after the swiftest storm.
I hear the echoes of the earth,
patterns,
stories.
They all carry me
like a wave,
lay me
in front of you.

Clothes Line

Sometimes words
are like clothes
on a line.
You have to let them breathe,
spend a little time
in the sunlight,
before
you use them...
so they fit,
convey what you're trying to say.
They smell so sweet,
she sees your vision too.

I sit here
everyone that walks through the door...
is a different version of you.
No matter the version,
difference,
feel...
your depth,
beauty,
feminine charm
pours through.
There is nothing that can mute
what is originally you.

Echo

I have bent over backwards...
being this,
that,
just right,
not enough,
believing it was a form of compassion,
connection.
When the curtain fell,
I realized
all any of us need
in those we love...
for each of us to be ourselves.
We choose each other,
bond,
experience life together
for a reason...
our souls heard an echo
that felt at home with ours.

Map

I lost my way once.
My mom died.
Seeing her in pain,
crying out,
delirious...
seeing a fierce fighter
on her knees...
my map disappeared.
The interesting thing,
all that blank space,
the beach view of what was...
I became creative with it.
I pieced together...
that abstract I mentioned (pg. 24).
When I found the strength
to dip into myself,
open myself up...
I pulled out these tools
I rarely took the time to fully see before.

Transform

Are you a tall lamp in a room?
Do you bring light,
like a life force?
Do you open your book,
you,
so it's clear...
how you developed
your own special way?
We create variations of recipes
based on another's.
And sometimes,
all a genius moment requires
is the right lighting.
Your unique sparkle matters,
it transforms.

Ladle

The world is a simmering pot
full of every tasty treat.
And you...
all you have to do is choose
the best ladle for you.

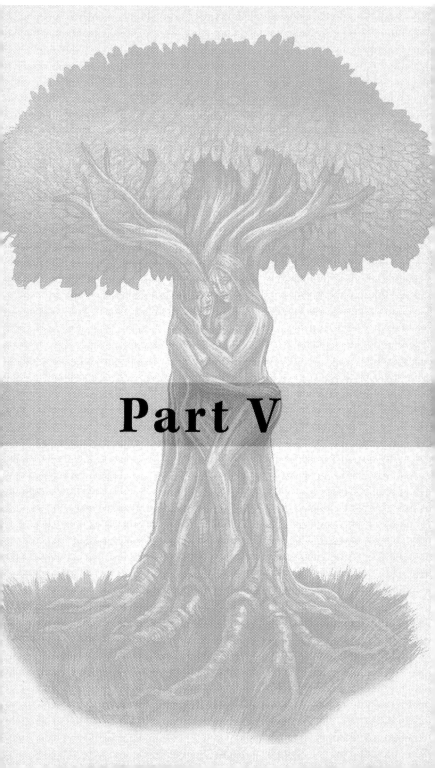

Part V

Fresh

Love is like cat nip,
we have to keep it fresh,
distribute it in varying amounts...
only use the best.
That'll get her rolling in the sheets,
showing her belly
purring non-stop!

Character

Each of us has that moment,
where we get that smile
spout off,
showing who we truly are.
Do it often.
Do it all the time.
Heck, sit at a coffee shop and watch...
simply through expression,
emotion
who's really letting it fly.
Be inspired,
those are the tables
where the person
they're with is captivated.

You Never Grow Old

Your heart beat is a novel.
It is a greeting card.
It is a wave
that washes ashore
parts of you,
ones you hide,
ones you share with me.
I could hear your novel
for a thousand years.

"Stay"

This morning could have been a blur
of getting ready,
I woke with a whisper,
a warm thigh,
a soft "hello",
"not yet",
"stay".
It's that perspective,
you.
Refreshing,
every angle
reminded I am beautiful.
I am everything I need to be
to be enough for me,
you,
us,
now, then, tomorrow, next week.

Seeing So Much More

Change is a pirouette,
revolution,
moment,
rest of our lifetime.
Change is experiencing lightning,
yet seeing so much more,
the kite,
key.
Change is sitting alone,
yet feeling crowded with love,
brimming with joy,
anticipating
our night together.
Change is opening up to the dawn,
love,
having you endlessly,
infinitely.
Change is a story that re-writes,
reconfigures destiny.

I Saw A Story

I saw a story
as I looked at you.
I saw the deep color
richness of your hue.
I saw little tiny things
that gave me every clue.
I saw that it's always been
ever will be
our link,
our 'I do'.

What if the famous 'thinker'
statue was a woman?
She got up
threw this image down,
breaking the mold,
admiring the cracks
with depth and sincerity...
depending on the viewer's angle,
her form morphed into a bear,
a tree,
whomever the heck she choose to be.

I Left A Trail

Look deeply my love,
look deeply inside of thee.
I left a trail,
we hiked together.
I made a notch in every single tree
That brings you to the top,
you can see us distinctively.

Beautiful

Tap,
Tap,
wake-up darn it,
it's me!
Let's go out!
It's raining that beautiful,
warm Summer rain.
I want to share it with you.
I want to laugh so long,
I don't care if we're sitting in mud.
I want to see you awake,
set yourself free.
Tonight shake off the leaves
from your beautiful tree.

Contagious Humor

I've found that showers
with you smell differently.
Our shampoos entwined haphazardly.
I find myself humming songs
get you to laugh.
It's done intentionally.
It sends you off with a smile.
Later in the day...
it sets the cat free from the
tree (removes fear),
if need be.

Soar

It is in the wind,
the air,
float of the waves,
waft of the sun's shine.
Love carries itself beyond,
returning to lift,
embrace
let go just enough,
so that which it loves flies.

We

We are the most beautiful bonsai tree,
deeply connected,
thoughtfully tended.
We share the sun,
life,
air,
knowing that each other's growth
feeds our own.

Confident

I bend
as if the wind can turn me
into a tree,
moving in synch
heaven's form of gravity.
I rise,
I rise
beyond history.
Legend knows
love shines bright
stands tall,
confident in its victory.

Imprints Without The Snow

There are places we go,
share,
just know.
I can see the remnants of you,
your glow.
My heart,
its imprint leaves tracks,
like in the snow.
It's my signal to you,
I'm here,
you can breathe now.
I won't let you go.

Rest Yourself On Me

I'll be your life raft,
rest yourself on me.
I'll be that person
that quiets the wind,
settles your sea.
I'll be that bird,
singing land is near,
there's hope,
look up...
I brought a branch
from our favorite tree.

Trust Yourself

Let go of what others perceive
of your perception of their perception.
They are the bricks,
the burden.
Shine as you.
Those first words,
that first impression,
your personal ink blot.
The way *you* want *your* world,
words to be.
Then, believe in *your* symphony.

[interestingly enough, this poem is
unintentionally shaped like a key hole}

Blurt It

You just showed me
the deepest part of you.
You shared a dream,
a layer you've barely
admitted to yourself.
It was a only a whisper before,
you blurted it out to me.
I've never seen you so beautiful,
vulnerable,
open,
enough for yourself,
and... most importantly,
happy.

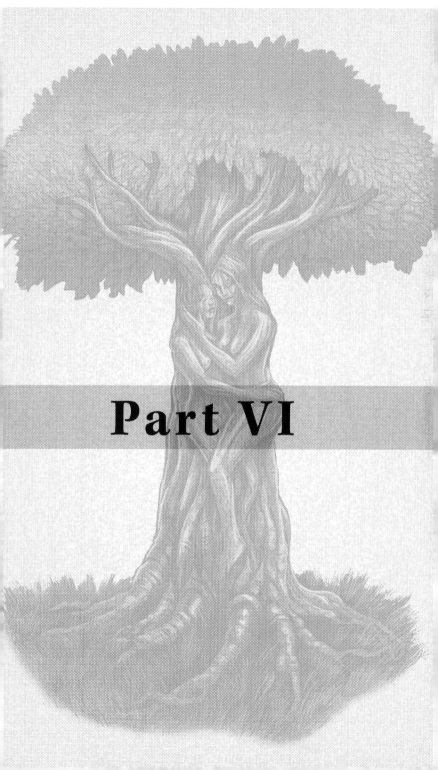

Part VI

She's Magical

Pick your color,
choose your song,
let it out...
burst out of that cage!
Feel those beautiful wings of yours
stretch so wide
you skim the edge,
then open them
beyond.
Realize the edge never existed.

Visionaries

The truth,
we create these illusions
of what having it together,
being gorgeous,
sexy,
wealthy...
consists of,
looks like,
based on what's around us,
instead of what's within.
What if,
what we're hiding,
that secret,
quirky talent (according to us)...
is exactly what the world needs?
Next time you wince at the
large woman in tights
or the less than perfect cross dresser,
consider this...
did you have that kind of
guts this morning,
to wear what you wanted,
do what you wanted,
say how you truly felt,
ask for what you need?
Our visionaries
are the ones that find their flow,

their version of love
and
bleed it beyond the river.
They irrigate the world.

Love Lingers

I've seen what the world can do.
I've seen the impact
each of us can make.
Love is a builder.
It creates the most amazing communities.
It lingers...
looking to extend its stay.
I know all of this is important to you.
It shows through
in everything you do.

There isn't a day that goes by, period.

I step into life
with you.
I don't let anything
slip away.
It's that depth of care...
which makes things real.

Words

Words are a battery pack,
they are the sun,
they can be the moon.
They can dress the people we love
in the warmest of clothes...
as they step into their day.
No matter the weather,
they feel the sun will continue to shine.
Love carries us far beyond the now.
Words are love's plane.
They make our map,
our destination,
dear,
memorable.

She rotates the world for me.
She's the seasons.
She's the leaves that populate my tree.
She's the soymilk in my tea.
She is the flavor,
the aroma...
all the warmth
life can be.

Change

What would it take
for us to grow
beyond this?
Beyond the boundary of fear,
beyond the enclosures we create,
duties,
the "how would I handle
this kind of change?
Would I be enough,
would it last,
would we last?"
What would you think
of this part of me?
Why would you love
this part of me,
when it's something
I can barely look at?
I do look at it...
because of you.
You look at it,
because you've always loved what you see.

Step

African American step dance,
demands attention,
respect.
It throws down fear,
grinds "I can't" under it's boots!
We all awaken
when we leave this kind of signature
on humanity's heart...
to never bow down (we are each royalty).
When you feel the passion,
love bubble up,
that burst of joy...
stand beyond the stars,
shine!
Even if you're the brightest,
biggest
and
that's scary for you.
Your light,
it's an Aurora Borealis,
a walkway for those around you.
It's an opening...
to a world worth discovering,
that is each of us.

We Move

I could sleep against you
for hours.
The rain outside,
it's your excuse to burrow.
You always have a reason to get close.
I love that about you.
Your need to love
be loved.
It surpasses fear,
insecurity.
You know my shards,
I know yours.
We move entranced
by how beautiful
we become regardless.

I Am A Lesbian

I'm not afraid of words,
you,
making mistakes.
I'm not afraid
of the shell I built,
cracked,
removed.
I'm not afraid,
who I was,
who I am.
I know
as I evolve,
I get ever more certain,
amazing,
true.
I can tear down walls,
foundations,
stand in the midst of it all,
confidently.
It's just space,
stuff.
It doesn't etch
who I am,
what I do,

now,
here.
What I did yesterday
does not become a part of me,
until I choose.

Roar Like The Ocean Waves

There are life-transforming choices
we make that significantly
magnify our power,
appeal,
belief in ourselves.
When we choose to love
ourselves so much...
that we roar like the ocean waves,
creating positive change,
it transforms us.
It leads others.
It leaves a wake in the world,
where people who need this,
flow in and are set free.
Lead with love.

Your Story

Never let anyone make you feel
things could have been worse...
what you experienced
wasn't a big deal.
Your experience,
version matters.
Consider the courage
it takes to re-write your story
into one of victory.
How can you make peace with what was...
shine the spotlight
on what you've become?
The bonsai tree is complex
and
beautiful in its simplicity.
Love carefully pruned
flowed into it.

I'm going to open up **the deepest part of me.**

I disappeared into a disguise.
I didn't even recognize it.
My disguise
kept repeating to give up
put it all to an end...
I never was enough,
it was my fault.
I thought it was my responsibility
to make everything better...
to make everyone around me bright...
even on the sunniest day,
it was...for me
the deepest,
darkest of night.
Something in me...
it stepped outside of me,
took a lingering look...
held me impossibly close...
for days,
weeks,
months...still.
It acts like a sponge,
cleaning up all the tears that
seep from every part of me.
I've been carrying this limp version of me...

trying to resuscitate,
awaken,
revive it.
I'm not afraid of what I see anymore.
I realize...a painter draws,
before she paints.
It's that love for myself,
my indomitable belief in who I am...
that's been carrying me.
There is light in this truth.

Escape Hatch

I lift you beyond now.
I remove that weight
you've been treading with.
We bouy each other with humor,
understanding
when the other needs rest.
Your voice carries me.
It stops the wind.
I help you tune into you.
I help you take everything off the desk.
It doesn't have to be solved now,
we can resolve it afterward.
Let's go be free.

What's so scary about "no"?
What's so scary
about imperfection?
What's so scary
about saying, "I love you?
Your lips hydrate my heart."

Hearing your morning shuffle,
feeling you slide back in bed,
wearing your **scent on me**...
never having this,
that's scary!

A wave is a mountain
with momentum
that delivers a kiss.
A wave finds so much peace
in its purpose,
it will ride a storm,
right itself,
continue as if nothing was amiss.

Silence

There we are
sitting quietly
beside each other.
The water is making more sound than us.
Yet, somehow
I can feel your heart beat,
hear your breathing,
experience your soul
wrapped around mine,
like a cloak to keep me warm,
safe.
Your unselfish love,
although a variation,
mirrors mine...
extended through you,
like a skilled weaver's tapestry,
helping you distinguish
what's stunning about our silence,
now.

The Best

The best thing I can do for
you this morning,
let you sleep,
recognizing your need to dive into you.
When you have so much love in your life,
it's nice to locate that nesting spot,
who you are at this moment,
enjoy it,
love it.
It smoothes out the wrinkles,
sets the table.
It prepares space to share.

Anywhere

I'd stop the ocean waves
mid-sentence for you.
I'd make that same ocean shallow,
just long enough,
you could walk right through.
That peaceful lapping shoreline,
the one you're drawn to...
I'd reconstruct it
anywhere in the world,
right here,
right now,
if it brought you back to you.

Printed in the United States
By Bookmasters